C000142278

SITTING ON THE FENCE

A Collection of Poetry
By
Emilie Lauren Jones

- - -

To Gayle + Kim

Best wishes,
Emilie

Published by Emilie Lauren Jones
Alpine Rise, Styvechale Coventry, CV3 6NT

© Emilie Lauren Jones 2012

All rights reserved.

This book is in copyright. No reproduction of any part
may take place without the permission of the author.

www.emilielaurenjones.co.uk

Printed in Great Britain by Newman Thomson,
West Sussex, England.

ISBN 978-0-9572253-0-5 Paperback

Emilie Lauren Jones lives in Coventry and has a BA Hons in English from Coventry University; she has been passionate about writing for as long as she can remember. Some of the fifty poems in this collection have been published in local magazines and newspapers or have won competitions. Emilie has previously been published by the Guardian Newspaper and Piccadilly Press as part of the anthology 'The Perfect Lie.' She published her first collection of poems with Chatterbox Publications in 2005, aged fifteen.

For my wonderful family, I am very lucky.

xxx

Sitting On The Pier

Sitting on the pier,
Because all are welcome here.
With their thoughts and dreams,
Their pasts and presents.
The sea air does not care
What mistakes you have made
Or will make.
The waters do not mind
If you are black or white or purple,
The sun and the rain
Do not discriminate,
They choose to fall equally on all,
Because they share this world.
The wood, rock, water, sand and cloud
Are content for me to sit with them
here in my denim shorts
and worn sandals.
To think, remember, imagine.
To mourn or to laugh,
Together or alone.
Healthy or struggling,
To stay for a day or a lifetime.
All are welcome here.

Anyone, Everyone, Anything

Six O'clock, it's morning,
Birds still snoring,
But I gotta wake up, face up
put on my makeup.
Knowing I could go anywhere,
Fly off to China,
Or just sit in the diner.
I could be anyone, everyone, anything.
But I've gotta have breakfast;
Toast, porridge
Or whatever's in the fridge.

I look out of my window,
See drizzle and a rainbow.
Clunk of the car key,
Excitement of the engine.

Stop by the travel shop,
When's the rain gonna stop?
Pick up a brochure,
Soon I could be in Beja,
Thank you, Obrigada.

Shortcut down the backstreets.
Guy pulls up, says 'get in.'
I walk away, ignore him.
And just as I'm questioning,
This lady drops her oranges,
Man picks them up, gives her a hug
and I remember that the world's good.

Feet trace the cobbles underneath me,
And I know that this will always be,
Even when I'm old
I'll see these streets in my soul.

Buskers outside the café,
Dreaming today's gonna be the day.
Maybe I could be a rockstar,
But first I'll need a red guitar.
Slip them some money,
Make a note in my diary.

Meet my friend at the café.
Hear her talk about her holiday.
Discus a new haircut,
one tea, two cups,
gotta go, drink up.

Remember her laugh
As I walk back to the car.
Man drops his shopping,
Reminds me of the oranges.
So I pick it up, walk away,
turn around to hear him say;
'Thank you for reminding me,
God bless, nice day.'

So I sit reading my book
Until I hear the lock jump.
Ruffled hair, ask what I want for tea.
Plates on laps, in front of the T.V.
Sorting out Corrie,
Solving murder mysteries.

Play games, have drinks,
'Till someone falls asleep.
Turn off before the news,
Go up to my own room.

Look at some photographs,
see the future and the past,
Written in my heart, in my soul,
No matter how old.

Just before I say goodnight,
See the sunset in the sky,
Give it my prayers,
My hopes and fears,
Feel the heat, feel the love,
A beating heart from God above.

Today was a good day,
I was anyone, everyone, anything.
But better than that –
I was me.

The Extremes of Twenty Ten

When their world collapsed
I was considering what to bet
on the one o'clock.
Then I went and had a shower,
while mothers searched for sons
and children searched for water
I was worrying what to wear tomorrow,
When the news came on
And I switched it off.
Something about a foreign country,
With a foreign lifestyle.
So I went to the pub
And we had to have our fags
outside. I think I noticed the sky.
Perhaps it was a starry night
which separated
two sides of human kind.
The fortunate and the desolate.
A head and a tail.
Sat on opposite sides of the world.
But sharing the same sky.
The burn and freeze of twenty ten:
The love of saving a singing child
and the reality of a broken state.

The Spider and the Flies

Inch by inch
It abseiled down and crawled back up,
Creating chains of sticky knots,
With eight black legs and
Eight black eyes
It dreamed its spidery dreams all night,
And crocheted its cartwheeled masterpiece
like perfect washing lines.

Next day I saw ensnared,
Three clumsy flies with web like hair,
Clawing and clamping them there.
 I stood and stared,
And could not bare,
The suffering they must be feeling
What if they had a mother?
Or another who wanted them
Back home?
Whilst they were here just waiting
To be ripped apart.

So with one quick swish of hand,
I tore the work of genius down,
Their faces, I think,
Were filled with glee
As they realised I had set them free!

A few days later,
After dinner,
I wandered past the webbed remains
And saw the spider clinging in vain

To what was left of what he'd made.
I noticed he was looking thinner
and tried to raise him from his slumber.
But as I poked and blew as well,
I realised he was now a shell.
I told him of my kindly act,
But he just stared, emptily back.

Gifts

Give me patience,
So I may teach.
Give me mystery,
So I may discover.
Give me kindness,
So I can inspire.
Give me freedom,
So I may speak.
Give me power,
So I can lead.
Give me strength,
So I can cope.
Give me happiness,
So I can share it.
Give me time,
So I'll make a difference.
Give me faith,
So I can believe.
Give me love,
So I will succeed.

My Room

A room. My room.
Four walls that know so much.
Just four walls.
But do they cry with me
when I sit alone?
Do they smile for me
When I stare at the stars?
And do they whisper
As I invite the sunshine in?

Once, slumped in the corner,
Laughing with friends;
There's still a stain on the carpet,
From where we spilt a drink.
Now I watch the flower bloom,
That we planted a year ago.
And the bed where so many dreams formed
And where fears strangled me in the darkness.

Hopes, dreams, memories, fears,
Enclosed in one box.
Two mirrors reflect dusk and dawn;
The excitement and anxiety of a new day
stares back at me when I glimpse them.
Four clocks. Each tells a different time;
One's an hour fast. Another holds a picture.
I hear their different ticks as I lie awake.

A city scarf hangs from the last match,
And a dress, still sparkling from the other
night.

I listen to the sound of Destiny,
As I dim the light
On these four walls
Just four walls.

A Grand Launch

Treading on stepping stones
towards the stage.
In Limbo –
back through the door
or forwards to the world?
Heart punching against my ribs,
sweating,
gasping,
choking,
walking on.
  A feast of expectant faces
hungrily waiting to feed
on a masterpiece
or a failure.
Journalists like Hyenas
already suggesting Headlines.
A button's pressed,
curtains open,
the rocket's launched.
But systems are shutting down
until it's just a charred stick
that clatters to the ground.
Fifteen minutes is up,
yet I want to say,
Ok. I just can't think,
But all my blank page says is:
'I've got writer's block.'

Learning at School

She said
"Come on in
Sit down class
Today we're going to practise Maths."
But because maths doesn't interest me
I looked outside
And learned to see
How ladies laugh
And how birds fly
And what deep blues God made the sky
I listened to the songs of trees
As the wind whistled through their leaves
And then she shouted
"Emilie!
Stop daydreaming and look at me!"

Walking Through Swanswell

Welcome to Swanswell.

Don't smile, just look ahead,
Don't answer when he calls me babe
and asks if I'm alright
and do I have a boyfriend
and have I got the time?

The sickly smell of weed and beer,
or worse, sitting in the atmosphere,
next to the three of them
who smoke and cheer
and leer and leer and leer

While the beggar and policewoman
have another conversation,
One that I don't understand,
And hope I never will.
Welcome to Swanswell.

Place of reconciliation,
Amongst the tank traps and blue paint,
That peels off the walls to reveal grey.
More grey and pebbledash,
False hopes put out by lit fag ash,
A place the phoenix long forgot.

But seriously, don't smile.
Just in case they think you're happy,
Or worse, looking at them funny.
Cos they'll wait for you on Tuesday

Night when orange lights are buzzing,
In the dark, they'll see you coming.
So keep your phone tight to your chest,
And by the way, can you run fast?
Or have you got the time yet?
Rewind it. Everyday,
Same faces, bags and prams,
Walking down the cycle lane.
No I don't have 20p.
Or a lighter. Sorry, call back later…
Have a lager, start a fire,
Mind the traffic, drop your litter.

No I haven't got the time, Sir.
                Welcome to the city centre.

Something More

Born in a barren winter land,
Where winds whisper across the earth
and snow settles on skeleton trees.
Stars sing amid metallic skies
and below, people shine in the darkness.

Time's so rich even money can't afford it,
Yet loving hands embrace it;
Turn it and watch sand trickle on.
Did they count down to Christmas then,
as we shout to ten to see the lights,
and reach to our souls to spark those candles?

In spring, seeds of ideas are planted
And soon begin to grow.
Look closely between pillars of grass,
See a forest of creatures;
Air pushing through every one,
A mass of life, a massive miracle,
That's so easy to step on and Destroy.

Children sit in the sunshine to watch T.V –
Colourful messages beamed from far away,
Characters crafted from the hands of writers
and appear just as planned.
Fun and morals moulded into something,
that we can understand.

But in the summer, listening to the radio;
Good News Is No News!
Is there too much to report?

Is it good that bad news shocks?
But sometimes it seems so lonely.
Until the thudding heartbeat of a train,
Or the laughter of the wind,
Serve as subtle reminders.

Still sometimes people doubt.
people are just people after all,
Even when a route's mapped out,
We still look for the shortcuts.
Yet still the summer sun pulsates,
And ideas that we planted mature
and evolve and all around is great.

On Autumn rivers where leaves float;
Tides guided by loving hands,
While shadows pass and mist moves on.
An art show attracts excited crowds
who see emotion splashed on every wall;
Images from the artists' soul.

Still some scientists sit determined
to prove it was all nothing more
than an accident.
Nothing more than luck,
That moons know how to fly around Jupiter
And that the rings of Saturn stay together Still.
They ignore fingerprints that traced their paths
On a night when stars collided in the black.

On My Beach

I've gone away for just a while,
Perhaps for the whole day.
I'll stumble through sand and rock
And watch the thoughtful waves.
Surrounded by the hush of beauty,
I shall stand for hours,
and let the day float by just like
the message in a bottle.
I'll tread the same path as the Walrus,
but the sand is fresher here.
I'll let the atmosphere breathe life,
And praise the sandy winds,
Let seaweed slip through my fingers,
And allow myself to grieve,
The passing of the sun,
As it moves to west from east.
Don't look for me as I proceed,
Along the cliff-top paths,
Accept today, I've gone away,
and one day I'll be back.

Living Ghost

Do you still remember me
Or am I just a memory?
Sometimes I think I can still see
That sparkle in your eyes.
And I wonder.
Do you remember
Those days in Genoa?
Standing, watching the boats go by.

A Blank Canvas

I am an artist.
My soft strokes caress the face of a woman.
I create no blemishes with my paint,
But her expression remains beautifully tragic,
Her eyes soft and determined,
Stare at their creator.

In silence
I build this other world,
Her dress is silk and she wears pearls,
But I still smudge the shadows round her eyes,
To highlight the pain she felt
A lifetime ago.

Carefully, precisely
I mould colours into shapes;
From nothing comes something.
I know every detail of her;
My hand designed her imperfections
And gave sunshine to her soul.

I am an artist.
And I paint the flowers in her room
A myriad of colours.
There is gold around her wrist,
But a realness in her eyes:
And that is why she is so beautiful.

Guessing That You're Gone

So here I am, at your place,
Where I know I shouldn't be.
Tears sitting on my fingertips
while I'm stuck at the wheel.
'Cos it's been almost a decade now,
since I was at your door,
And I'm guessing
that you're not here anymore.

Your curtains are not drawn,
Your ornaments are gone,
The flowers aren't as beautiful
And the sun is getting cold.
The world turned round,
Reflections changed,
Still I'm begging, yes
I'm begging, please
bring it back to me.

The purple paint is peeling
But the colour's still unchanged,
I smile at the memories,
and cry at all the pain.

I'm trying to ring your phone,
To tell you that I'm home,
But I'm guessing now,
I'm guessing
that you're gone.

Between The Sand and Sea

Sitting on a rock,
In the middle,
Of the sea and sand.
Both analyse
a different angle.
"Take my hand,"
Says the sand,
"Come with me,"
Says the sea.
It's said they used to touch, you know,
Not that you'd believe it now.

It's funny how beauty's made so differently.
Yet I prefer neither sand nor sea.
And why should I?
Can you not be wet and dry
at the same time?
Still, the sea waves at me
and the sand holds out it's hand.
While I wonder how the sea could ever
understand,
What it feels like to walk the land,
And how the sand could ever see,
How much like flying floating can be.

Then the wind blows,
and a mixture of salt and grit,
makes my eyes sting.
So they both retreat,
Thinking what they've done to me.
Although inside I'm so amused,

Just wondering in the moonlight,
How one set of words
can have two different tunes.

I'm Not Gone

I'm not gone,
I'm still the same person I was before.
When you walk down the street,
I'm one step behind.
When you watch the television,
I still sit by you're side.
I listen to your conversations,
Laugh at your jokes,
And smile as you remember the good times.

I'm not gone,
I'm the breeze that rustles the trees in our
garden.
When you cry I put my arm around you,
I join in when you sing our songs.
I sit at the end of your bed at night,
And when you wake up,
I'm still there.

I'm not gone,
I'm just waiting.
This is not the end, just a new chapter,
I dance next to you at parties,
When you're happy, I'm happy.
I sit in the back seat of the car,
I'm the reflection in the window,
And I hold open the door.

I'm not gone.
So don't stop being you, carry on.
If you meet someone new,

I'll still hold your hand.
I'm always with you, by your side.
I still breathe in your perfume,
And run my fingers through your hair.
Soon we'll be together,
But until then,
 Take care.

Colour Blind

He sees the world in black and white,
No in between, just day and night.
No in between, just wrong and right.

He wakes.
Opens his eyes from the black,
And sees white light slowly coming back.
The blackbirds sing sweetly in the trees,
The white doves sit silently next to these.

But still he doesn't see inbetween.
And he thinks that trees are only green.
From his eyes no shades can be seen.
Shame he'll never see what they mean.

He'll never hear a magpie calling,
Never hear a piano playing.
Won't see there's more than black or white,
Day or night, wrong or right.

He will not see a bigger picture,
He will not see them work together,
Mixing, making beautiful songs.
He only sees what's right or wrong.

Think of Me

Don't think of me in black and grey,
But as forests and the oceans spray,
lemons ripening in the sun,
rivers racing, calm and still.
Remember redness in my cheeks,
after standing in the breeze
or from long walks in the snow -
Remember me, the one you know.

Don't dream of me in black and grey.
Think of me as strawberries,
and raindrops glistening in the trees.
Remember orange in my laugh,
and pansies, pinks and violets.
Don't picture me in black and grey,
that's not who I was or am today.

Don't see me as a ghostly shadow,
or something that you just imagine,
Don't see me as black and grey,
not now, tomorrow or yesterday.
Remember gold in my kisses,
turquoise music, silver wishes,
beating hearts as we cuddled,
aqua reflections in purple puddles.
All I ask – remember me,
who I was and will still be.

We Will Smile

I'd tell you that I'd die for you,
but it's such a cliché,
and too easy anyway.
It's harder for me
to let you leave,
or even consider the possibility
that one day you won't be
there
on your favourite chair,
when I walk in the room,
because, like lightning, time,
smashed through too soon
and left broken change.
But still, I'll tell you anyway,
how I would steal all your pain
to keep sweet destiny away.
But either way,
we will see happiness again;
you will smile
and I will laugh
as if no time
had ever passed.

My Confessions

Yes, it was me,
Who put your iPod in the wash,
Who hit the wall
And then drove off.
That smashed the light,
While playing on the Wii,
I did it all,
Yes, it was me!
I hid the mess in the wardrobe,
It's my fault the door doesn't close.
And all those glasses that disappeared,
Which I said you'd lost over the years.
The broken eggs, the lost passport,
The missing handle on the door,
The Busted CD that's now in half,
I'm the criminal at large!
Burnt tea towels, ripped wall paper,
Ashes from a fireworks taper,
Stained windows, mascara smears,
Your trainers I said I'd never wear,
Orange hair dye in the bath,
Milk that turned the kettle black,
Yes, Yes! I did all that!
So to you now I will confess,
To get these events off my chest...
Or maybe I'll throw this list away?
And tell you all another day...

Scarlet Ribbons

She walks along old Scarlet Bay,
Wondering why he went away.
Staring into sweet abyss,
Thoughts of kisses that she'll miss.
With gentle skin and smoky hair,
And scarlet ribbons tied with care.

No more letters sealed with kisses,
No fairytales or granted wishes.
No more will he hold her hand;
She walks alone across the sand.
Her heart drowning in the pain,
Never will it mend again.

For him her soul is calling, calling,
Just like he did falling, falling.
So much sadness in those eyes,
So, so many tears she's cried.
With her heart that's good and fair,
And scarlet ribbons in her hair.
She watches more ships sail away,
Heading far from Scarlet Bay.

About The Writer

At night she sits alone,
Writes another song or poem.
Spills her feelings on the page.
Lets her fears fall away.
And they always say;
"How do you write so well?
Is there some sort of magic spell?"
But they don't know it's all her dreams,
All her tears and her screams,
All her sunshine, all her rain,
All her love and all her faith.
They just see a story or a song.
But they have got it all so wrong.
And she's known it all along;
She's not a writer, just a fake;
She writes because she's kept awake.
She doesn't make these stories up,
If you intimately look,
Her life's not as perfect as it seems
And she's not as great as you believe.

Dear Bully

Remember me?
A soul behind a pair of eyes
That you were happy to despise
Listening to my tortured cries
And silent tears that filled my eyes
Just a victim of your highs
A player in your great disguise
Another fatality to your lies
So many faults to sensationalise
And I came up with no replies
No one would stop this great demise
No friendly faces or allies
Every day a sad reprise.

Remember me?

Now I have the upper hand
But unlike you I don't command
Or work on 'friendships' to expand
There are no jokes or sneers pre-planned
I will not leave you in no mans land
Because I experienced that first hand
And as far as I understand
No one has the right to demand.

I am happy I am free
God answered my heartfelt plea
And a better person you now see

So now do you remember me?

In The Clearing

She likes the way the water trembles
when she dips her fingers, just a little
and feels the wet upon her skin,
whilst comforting heat gathers it in.
She wonders if she extended further,
Diving in completely, swallowed
By the suffocating blur of sereneness,
Would it matter?

She does not know that He is there,
Watching every thought.
Silently, He breathes her pain,
in her dark. Which to Him is light.
Underneath a sky
Of stars and stars and stars.

To her the world right now
is this clearing in the woods.
Protected by mud and sticky leaves,
Heat from a summer's sleepy sun,
A breeze. In summers slumberous haze.
Her gaze, fixed upon the water
And she wonders
Whilst His love surrounds her.

The Witches Glasses

I'm told there's a pair of magic glasses
Somewhere on this earth.
That always show the wearer truth;
Though I'm told the truth may hurt.

The tale goes that wearer one,
A miserable old man.
Bought them off a wise old witch,
From a market east of France

It's said a month or two had passed
When he saw the witch again.
"So tell me Sir," the kind witch said,
"Your truths you did attain?"

"I saw the world for what it was,"
Said the grim and pale man,
"All my beliefs I've had confirmed,
I now know how right I am.

This earth is full of liars and cheats,
Of scoundrels and of crooks.
I saw suffering and pain,
In every place I looked."

Later on that day;
Or so the story goes.
He gave the glasses to another man,
Who he thought should see the truth.

That other man was grateful,
Already happy and content,
He saw only love and beauty,
Everywhere he went.

He returned them to the first man,
With a smile upon his face.
He told him exactly what he saw,
And how the world was great.

The first man stared in disbelief
And anger filled his face.
"How can you see this world as good
When that is not the case?"

So he went to find that wise old witch;
To put her in her place.
To tell her that the glasses lied
And to have them back again.

It's said she never answered back,
She just smiled and she sighed.
For as the sweet, white-witch knew well;
The glasses never lied.

Forgiveness

I wonder how it feels to die,
To let all hurt just slip aside,
to take away my bleary eyes
and let me see just like a child.
Before the world stamps pre-conceived ideas
on their mind
and lets them think that they are right.

I wonder how it feels?
To let all hopes be healed,
to hear rainbows calling once again,
just like bells when you were young.
I wonder if it makes you cry,
to leave such anger behind
and learn to walk on trust instead.
Oh, must we wait till we are dead?

Curriculum Vitae

Why should you hire me and
Not all the other ones,
Who've sent you little letters
Applying for a job?

I didn't get all A*'s,
In fact I sometimes turn up late,
I don't even own a diary,
Remind me, what's the date?

But I could be your Wonder Woman,
I could make us money,
I just need you to notice,
And to place your faith in me.

Well would you love me baby
if I was on the stage,
Smeared in glitter gels,
PVC and vodka dreams?

Or I could be so good to you,
And cook you all your meals,
wear a nice white apron
and nod at everything.

Perhaps I might confuse you,
You can't wrap me in a box,
I am me, I am unique,
And that is what I've got.

Ceiling Tiles

Have I seen this place before?
Things seem so familiar.
Once upon a time in a dream?
Or was it in reality?
Or is it now that I really dream?
I lie awake and count the hours,
But to what I do not know.
When I shake and scream
She comforts me,
And tells me to be strong.
But the mind is such a powerful thing,
It's hard to fight it off.
Blackness often descends then lifts
It sometimes comes with rain.
Then when she holds me in her arms,
It sometimes goes away.
She doesn't sleep,
She thinks of me,
So I pretend I'm fine.
I focus on the ceiling tiles,
And the patterns that I find
Swirling, mixing, shaking, rocking
Round and round they go.
So I watch them day or night,
Whenever I feel low.

Between These Spires

I walk the streets between these spires.
Knowing every nook and cranny;
Every place to hide.
Following the footsteps of ghosts
From the past.
Who walked these steps a thousand times.
Feeling every stone beneath their feet,
Hiding behind forgotten walls,
Listening out for horses hooves,
And the toll of bells.
Pulling their hats on tight,
Through the mist
Finding a doorway
And following a hundred others.
Now I follow their steps alone.
Between these spires,
I walk the streets.
Following the steps
Of a thousand ghosts.
Listening to the toll of bells.
Through the metal railings of a doorway
In the mist.

Just Another Day

Remember how we skated,
With snow flakes in our hair,
Christmas lights, hot chocolate dreams
Lighting up the air,

Well give me one more Christmas
And another birthday too,
Give me just another day,
Where I don't know the truth.

Lets pretend that you untold me,
And carry on today,
As if things hadn't altered;
It's just another day.

The snow has now stopped falling,
The ice begins to crack,
So hide all your analysis,
Please put away your scans.

I'll live under chocolate clouds,
Believing life goes on.
All I ask, is let me stay
Another day – just one.

Another day of ignorance,
Full of normalities,
Before the ice swallows this life
And blows my chocolate's steam.

On The Tube

They travelled along in strange silence.
Rushing people. In and out.
Staring at aliens from the same world.
Staring but never seeing.
Just waiting to get off.

One man despising music
Played by the boy on his left.
Staring at the shoes
Of the lady to his right.
Why did she wear those shoes today?

He sees an article in the paper,
On Nazi Germany.
So detached from today's world,
He thinks.
Soldiers shoving people like cattle;
Staring and hating them for being born.
Their victims staring back;
Despising their captors.
Thrown onto trucks
And paraded around the streets.
Just waiting to get off.

A woman on the tube
Watches a man with a newspaper;
Irritated as he rustles it.
She wonders why the lady on her left
Brings her toddler on the tube at this time.

She notices a poster for a film

About the slave trade.
How different from today;
She thinks.
Pushed like animals onto ships.
The sailors ears burn from their songs,
Judging them for being born.
The captured hating their captors.
Staring at each other in mutual disgust.
Waiting for the ship to stop,
Just waiting to get off.

On the tube.
Packed like tuna, swaying
against each other
Used to the strange silence,
The warm rush of air
As the doors open and shut.
Just waiting to get off.

War Symphony

Some man – politician?
Says play, we listen
And the people down there
Start to dance
To the music, to the rhythm.
To the pace of the guns,
To the beat of the bombs.
This club gets cramped
Starts to sweat, alcohol,
Or better yet rotting flesh.
Hear the hate in their eyes,
Bitter taste of goodbyes.
Fighting ideologies with guns
But what's wrong
Opinions or actions?
Crash of symbols
Crashing statues
Posters shouting
Children doubting
What's to come.
So pass me a gun
And I'll dance
To destruction.
Green shadows crawling
The Longest night's coming.

Forever Mine

In life we are not meant to be.
Two souls, kept apart by fate.
So now I keep you in my head,
And dream of you when I sleep.

Two paths that were not meant to cross,
Two hearts never supposed to meet,
Two hands never allowed to touch;
Except for in our dreams.

So many wasted tears I cried,
As we were torn apart.
No one else thought we should stay
Together, in each others arms.

Now all I have is memories,
And although this may seem unfair,
I have you now all to myself;
You're kept inside my head.

And I only remember happy times,
Not times you made me cry.
And I mould you into who I want,
So our hands will stay entwined.

So now our lips and skin may touch,
Because no one knows or minds,
That I am forever yours my love,
And you, forever mine.

Words, Words, Words

Comfort me and rescue me,
Crush me and destroy me.
Excite me and enthral me,
Reach for me and hold me.
Stay in my mind forever,
Don't leave me or get old.
Dance like rays of bright white lights,
Grow wings and over time take flight.
Love me and entice me,
In your passion you will bind me.
Words, so great and mighty,
Crafted and decided
How can you be *just* words?

Perpetual Eternity

My weary heart begins to slow,
And my body starts to tire.
So my sleepy eyes start to shut
On this world for a final time.

Now Lord, I'm lying, dying here,
And I think of all you gave.
And I'm begging, Lord, I'm begging,
Please don't take it all away.

But my restless soul does as it's told;
And I leave this world behind.
And Lord, you're still holding my hand
As I realise I've arrived.

So finally I meet my love,
And we walk always hand in hand.
We walk by never ending seas,
On never ending sands.

And we go towards your kingdom,
With its ruby and gold walls.
And I'm crying Lord, I'm crying,
With joy, at what I behold.

Your kingdom and your children, Lord.
Their souls are filled with ease.
Your kingdom and your children, Lord.
And one of them is me.

The Unloved

Just half a ghost in a doorway,
not alive, not dead; I'm the unloved.
Dumped amongst the people's feet,
in corners where their sick still clings
to empty bars and cash machines.

But now it's not just me, it's you;
the drug drumming through my veins.
Sometimes I dream they let you stay,
that your best chance could be with me.

'Cos they don't really care for us,
they're just paid to give a damn
about the scum that's on their list;
like me a 'wasted ex-druggie' –
unloved, forgotten residue,
residing on the people's streets,
in cracks they hate to think exist.

Still, even I can dream and wish:
To kiss and warm you in my arms
be the one you need and love.
Imagine that we'll always stay,
two heartbeats, away from them,
you swelling safely deep inside,
where snaking fingers cannot reach.

But I know they'll come and soon I'll scream
I'll scream in pain from death not birth,

when snipers find and shoot us down.
To save you from a sickening beast –
An unloved, homeless mother. Me.

Streets Made of Glitter

The ground is made of glitter,
and it's not very stable.
Your heels sometimes stick in
And you start to find you're sinking.
If you knock on a door
there's often no one in it.

Because they're out at a party,
Drinking diamonds and Bacardi.
Smiles don't come free here,
But you see them in the papers.
Too submerged by life to live it,
Too in love with love to give it.

Glitter's slippy when it rains,
Here, take this. Relieve the pain.
Maybe sell your story,
Hold the money, hold the glory.
 Is it familiarity you see?
Were they just friends or family?
It takes too long to remember,
in a street that's made of glitter
but you see it everyday
in the papers.

Clocks

My two hands will never feel you,
My face will never see into yours.
I just walk on.
Reliably counting every second.
I am your friend and I heal you,
I am your enemy and I pass you by.
And sometimes in the dead of night,
I comfort you or wake you,
As I count as time goes by.
Change me or ignore me,
I will never lie.
I scare you and I haunt you,
And count to sixty when you cry.
Eternity and forever,
Seem unimaginable to you,
But I've been here since never
And I'll be here until then too.
Don't ever try to track me;
I'm good at playing games.
People just can't forget me;
They waste so many days.
And all because I tick along,
To count the time away.

Make Me Love You

I see the way you look at me
And I can't help but smile.
You know all the lines from my favourite films,
And buy me my favourite wine.
You're handsome and you're funny,
And best of all you're kind,
You offered out your heart to me
And all you want is mine.

So when you asked to marry me,
It was kind of rude to laugh,
But I just can not be with you
Without that special spark.
It's annoying that you're clever, yet
you still cant make me see,
how you and I could live together, forever
happily.
Why can't you make me love you?
It's really quite unfair.
I know that you'd be decent
and we'd make a pretty pair.
We like all the same music,
We like all the same food,
But when you put your hands on me,
I'm just not in the mood.

If only I could make me love you,
It would be so good…

Unnecessary Rules

So I start my sentence with
A capital letter.
Because you told me to.
And yes, some rules
are necessary.
But some exist
TO
B   M
O   E
X
IN

Well,
I'd like to
B
R
E
A
K
through
your red tape walls.
Run through it and open
up the way
to a
sensible place.
Where I can
vote on rules
that you enforce on me.
Yes. It's good to live
in a free
country

A Reality

So break, break me,
I'll stay inside these lies still.
Just wait, race me,
There's more to life than winning.

You say, you'll see;
I will no doubt about it.
So walk, walk free,
I'll break these chains without you.

Perfection's not real,
I'm sorry you were lied to.
Just turn to face me,
Bring yourself to see the danger.

The weight, is real,
How are you gonna change things?
All that, you feel,
You can't just hide forever.

Don't waste, your life,
I've heard it all before you.
So deep, the knife,
It twists and moves right through me.

Perfection's not real,
I'm sorry you were lied to.
Turn your face to me,
Bring yourself to see the angles.

This is, my life,
I see it all unfolding.
This time, is mine,
Just watch my hands create it.

So go, leave me,
I will cope for a minute.
Play cards, drink tea,
Watch dragons soar above me.

Perfection's not real,
I'm sorry you were lied to.
Lift your face and see,
It's better than you could believe.

In The Dock

I used to watch dem gangsta's loads,
Bangin' tunes, ridin' dirty down the slip roads,
Always wit a new girl an monies by da case
load.
I used to fink "dats wot I deserve, dats wot I is
owed;"
So I fort, I cud see ma way down to Silk Road.
I knew dat it weren't gonna cum easy,
"Der is always a price to pay" So ma old man
used to say.
I jus neva fort it wud end up dis way.

I member dat fir time when I hooked up wit KG;
An he learned me how to work dem ladies,
An gave me ma fir taste a weed.
He said like "blood, dis is da life fir me;"
And I agreed;
  Dis was wot I wanted, dis was ma dream.

 I wore ma ices wit pride, I wos irie.
Yeh, I slotted a few peeps along da way,
But dat aint really nothing in dis games play.
 Used to hang in da shadows wit ma homies.
Drinkin Vodka, wit da hood; dey got to know
me.
Dey wanted me, dey fort I was safe, see.
 Knew I had to do sumfin to let it be,
But I swear blood, I neva meant to agree;
Not to sumin like dis, it jus ain't me.

But once I was in wit dem, I was in wit da plan.

See, I ain't no ditcha or no grass man.
Dey said "you do dis or we send you to Him;"
I knew wot dat meant, blood; it was you or me,
I wasn't in no position to disagree.
I wos already caught up in da debris,
Cos I ain't no member of the bourgeoisie.
I jus knew dat it cudn't be me.

I still hear da scream, see his face as he called ma
name,
He said; "blood, do da right fing, don't be
ashamed."
But wot is da right fing in dis screwed up game?
It wos da wrong peeps dat he messed wit,
Tho still can't believe it wos me dat dun it,
I jus pulled da trigga' an in a instant I finished it.

Now I see dat dis ain't right, to steal life from
anotha',
But it's to late for me and ma blood bruva',
We got caught up in a war, now I killed anotha'.
An I'm here makin' excuses to 'is motha',
Tellin' her; "life's tough;" like KG used to tell
me.
But she already knows, probably more dan me,
Suddenly I hear wot da judge is sayin': "Guilty."

Love

Love. Why do you hurt me?
Love. Why do you make me cry?
Love. why do you kill me,
When I have to say goodbye?
Love. Why can't you love me,
And never cause me pain?
Oh love. Love me forever.
And I will do the same.
Love. Even if you hurt me,
There's nothing else more true.
So love, forever guide me,
And love will see us through.

The Rainbow Painter

I'm outside, it starts to rain,
The summer sun, he hides his face.
The rainbow spreads across the sky,
Reminder of lifetimes gone by,
And promises that never die.

So many fates held in those hands;
Older than the world itself,
And the artist of all man.
The One who guides the stars at night,
Who draws the rainbows in the skies.

In our multicoloured world,
We watch miracles occur;
Birds fly and flowers grow,
He draws on the love we know.
Watched over by a billion eyes,
He paints rainbows in the skies.

English Rose

My English Rose, who stands on the cliff edge,
And looks across beyond the sea,
Past the horizon,
To a place you'll never go.

Tied down by your roots,
The one's that hold you to this English soil.
A part of you that grasps so tightly
To a land you know and love.

But fresh petals
Stretch out
Reaching for another place.
And your mind soars to the sun.

Your roots and your name,
Hold you back.
Nature will not let you go,
Is it frightened of something new?

My English rose, why don't you go?
Find happiness somewhere else,
And then come home,
And sing sweet songs from far off lands.

Nature made you beautiful,
So why do you suffer so?
My English Rose, don't feel bad.
Don't let your roots, your name
or nature, hold you back.

True Love

You said you wanted two kids,
I said I'd quite like three.
You said it didn't matter
Because you loved only me.
Your skin as rich as coffee,
Your voice so strong and soft
Your lips that left a tingle
Wherever they had touched.
You said that you liked dancing,
I said that was cool.
You said that you'd quite like it,
If I could dance with you.
I said that I liked reading,
You said that you did too,
And your eyes smiled like sprinklers
when they catch the sun.
Then you took me in your arms and
Told me about love.
So it's a shame
I never knew your name
Because we were both drunk.

At The Crossroads

Looking back
I see a path of destruction:
Simmering flames and raging fires;
Lasting effects of my desires.
Grasping guiltily at what I craved,
Destroying souls along the way.
Stolen treasures are now mine,
But so is a conscience burned by fire,
As lust not love was my desire.

I stand here, all alone,
At a fork in the road.
It's not too late to make amends;
I see that on the road that bends.
But the other path is long and straight;
It goes downhill – an easier way?
Money grows instead of flowers,
And status stands taller than trees.
But which do I desire of these?

On one track the sun shines all day,
But isn't that how fires are made?
And with the heat comes a great thirst,
And more heat makes it worse and worse.
So if I take the other course,
Can I still achieve it all?
Do love and faith and honesty,
Bring the power to succeed?

Its hard to tell as I stand here
At the crossroads.

Should I hope love never tires
Or do I trust those tempting fires?

Growing Pains

My Baby.
I held you in my arms,
Saw your first smile,
Stared into your eyes.
And I promised I'd protect you.
I thought the sun would always shine,
I thought I'd make life perfect,
I thought you'd never shed a tear,
Because I'd hold your hand forever.

Now you've grown up much more,
We often walk together.
But today a bird fell from a tree
And landed on the floor.
Its little eyes span all around
Until they closed forever.
You looked at me and asked me "why?"
I struggled for an answer.
I told you how God's plans seem strange,
But to trust there is a reason.
That tiny bird would now fly freely
On and on forever.
He will fly beyond the sun,
Past all our fantasies.
You nodded like you understood.
I think perhaps you did.

Act Six

In fair Verona we no longer laid our scene,
Less like star-crossed loves,
More like loves young dream.
After we escaped, my Romeo and me.

Our lips did lots of praying,
Our hands were free as gloves,
laughter sweet like roses,
watched by jealous stars above.

Two households alike in bitterness
Still fought a desperate war.
Pointing swords of blame,
Blood betrayed by blood.

Our new friends showed us kindness,
They welcomed us to their dance
And that was when I saw him
Give her loves first glance.

Now alone upon our balcony
From up high I see him hiding,
He calls out for her crying;
"Did my heart love till now?"

Tempt not a desperate woman,
I was just one more Rosaline,
So I hear the stage coach coming
and lie waiting for the wheels.

Amelia's Song

Red, red dress
And blue, blue eyes,
Your words like daisy chains
made me smile.

I knew it could just last a while,
But you changed my life
with your silly thoughts of paradise.
Those organised dreams of lullabies
with faith and love that got you by.

From 6pm on frosty nights
To 8am and morning skies
I promised you I'd never lie
You promised me Helios' light.

Though I turned and walked away
I will love you every day,
Amelia
My loyal friend,
I promise you it's not the e…

Poems Listed Alphabetically